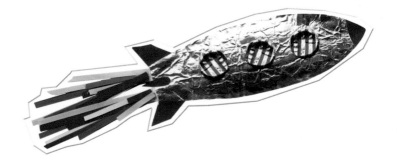

BLAST OFF!
THE MOON

Helen and David Orme

ticktock

Copyright © ticktock Entertainment Ltd 2007
First published in Great Britain in 2006 by ticktock Media Ltd.,
Unit 2, Orchard Business Centre, North Farm Road,
Tunbridge Wells, Kent, TN2 3XF

ticktock project editor: Julia Adams
ticktock project designer: Emma Randall

We would like to thank: Sandra Voss, Tim Bones, James Powell,
Indexing Specialists (UK) Ltd.

ISBN 978 1 84696 047 5
Printed in China
A CIP catalogue record for this book is available from the British Library.

Picture credits
t=top, b=bottom, c=centre, l-left, r=right
Alamy: 15cl, 15br; NASA: 1tl, 1br, 6, 7tr, 7br, 8, 11cl, 11br, 12cl, 12br, 16cr, 17tl, 17br, 18, 19tr, 19bl, 20, 21tr, 21bl, 22, 23tl,
23br; Science Photo Library: 4/5bg (original), 9tr; Shutterstock: front cover, 2/3bg, 7tl, 16cl, 24bg; ticktock picture archive: 5tl,
6/7bg, 9br, 10/11bg, 10, 11tr, 13tr, 13bl, 14/15bg, 14, 15tr, 15bl, 18/19bg, 11/13bg;
Every effort has been made to trace the copyright holders, and we apologise in advance for any unintentional omissions.
We would be pleased to insert the appropriate acknowledgements in any subsequent edition of this publication.

Contents

Where is the Moon? 4-5

Moon Facts 6-7

On the Surface 8-9

The Far Side 10-11

The Moon's Shapes 12-13

The Moon and Earth 14-15

Water on the Moon? 16-17

Men on the Moon 18-19

Moon Landers 20-21

Travel and Life on the Moon 22-23

Glossary and Index 24

Where is the Moon?

There are eight planets in our **solar system**. The planets travel around the Sun. Some planets have **satellites** called moons. The Earth has one moon.

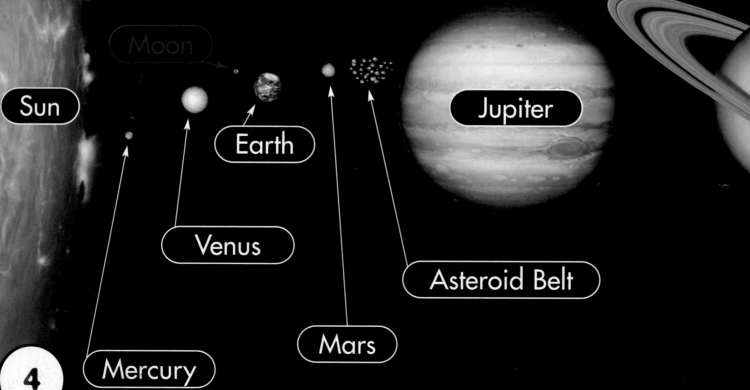

Moon

Sun

Earth

Jupiter

Venus

Asteroid Belt

Mars

Mercury

The Moon's orbit

The Moon travels around the Earth about every 27 **Earth days**. This journey is called its **orbit**.

Pluto

Saturn

Neptune

Uranus

Kuiper Belt

Moon Facts

The Moon is much smaller than the Earth. It has no **atmosphere** and no life. The surface of the Moon hasn't changed for millions of years.

This is the surface of the Moon. It is rocky, dry and dusty.

12,756 kilometres

Earth

5,594 kilometres

Moon

The Moon is less than
half the size of the Earth!

Like the Earth, the
Moon is always
spinning.
The time it takes for
a moon or planet to
spin around once is
called a day.
One day on the
Moon is about 27
Earth days long!

Moon

On the Surface

Look at the Moon through binoculars or a telescope. You will see that it has mountains, flat plains, and lots of **craters**.

crater

The craters on the Moon were made millions of years ago. Huge rocks flying through space crashed into the Moon and left craters on its surface.

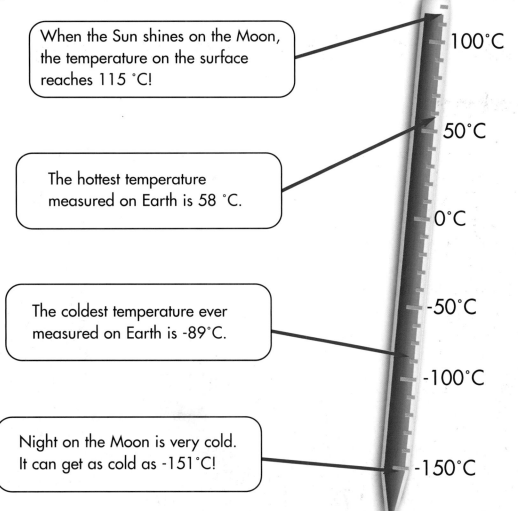

When the Sun shines on the Moon, the temperature on the surface reaches 115 °C!

The hottest temperature measured on Earth is 58 °C.

The coldest temperature ever measured on Earth is -89°C.

Night on the Moon is very cold. It can get as cold as -151°C!

100°C

50°C

0°C

-50°C

-100°C

-150°C

The Far Side

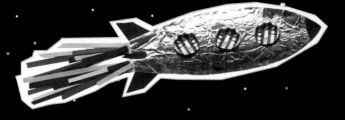

The same side of the Moon always faces the Earth. That is why early **astronomers** had no idea what the other side of the Moon looked like.

This picture shows the Earth with the Moon. The side which is not facing the Earth is called the Far Side of the Moon.

In 1959, Russia launched the Luna 3 spacecraft. It took the first pictures of the Far Side of the Moon. This is a drawing of Luna 3.

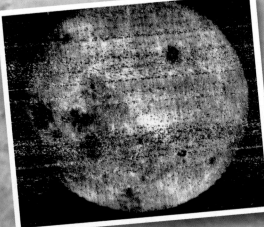

This photograph of the Far Side of the Moon was taken by Luna 3 in 1959.

This photograph was taken in 1990 by the Galileo spacecraft. It shows that the Far Side of the Moon has many **craters**.

The Moon's Shapes

When we look at the Moon from Earth over a few nights, it looks like it is changing shape. This is because we can only see the part of the Moon that the Sun is shining on.

Sometimes we can see all of the Moon. We call this a full Moon.

Sometimes we can only see half of the Moon.

Sometimes we cannot see the Moon at all because of its position in space. This is called a new Moon.

As it moves around the Earth, different parts of the Moon's surface are lit up by the Sun. The blue line on each Moon picture marks the part we can see from Earth.

Moon in orbit

full Moon

Earth

new Moon

sunlight

full Moon

new Moon

These photographs show how the Moon seems to change into different shapes during one month.

The Moon and Earth

The Moon is in **orbit** around the Earth. This is because a special force holds the Moon and the Earth together in space.

Moon's orbit around Earth

The special force also affects what happens on Earth. It creates the **tides** in the Earth's seas and oceans.

As the Moon moves around the Earth, the force pulls the water from oceans and seas slightly towards the Moon.

We call this high tide.

high tide

At the same time, the water levels drop in other places where the force does not reach.

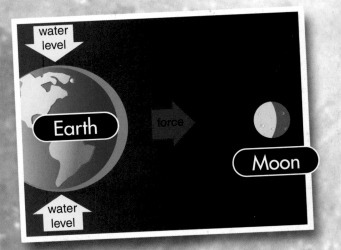

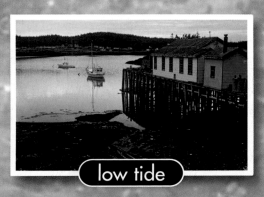

low tide

We call this a low tide.

Water on the Moon?

Scientists used to think that the Moon was completely dry. But now they think there may be as much as 6 billion tonnes of ice at the Moon's North and South Poles!

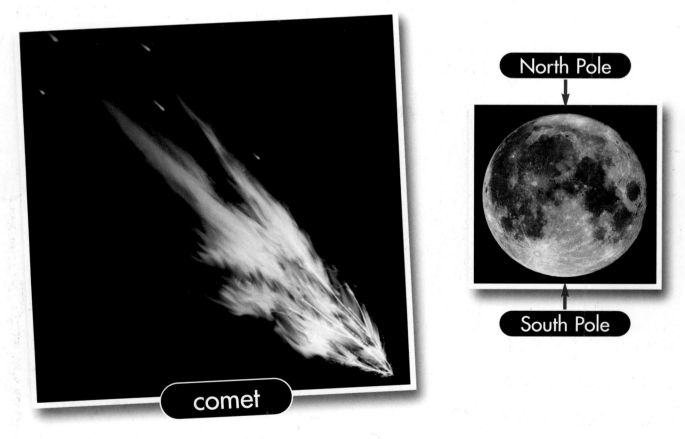

comet

North Pole

South Pole

The ice probably reached the Moon when **comets** hit its surface. Comets are mainly made of ice.

deep crater

The ice from the comet doesn't melt because it is lying in deep **craters**. It is probably covered with Moon dust. The Sun's heat never reaches these places.

This frozen water could be very useful if people ever wanted to live on the Moon!

This is a painting of a **moonbase**. The frozen water would be used as drinking water.

Men on the Moon

The Moon is the only place in space that people have visited. Six **Apollo** missions have successfully landed on the Moon.

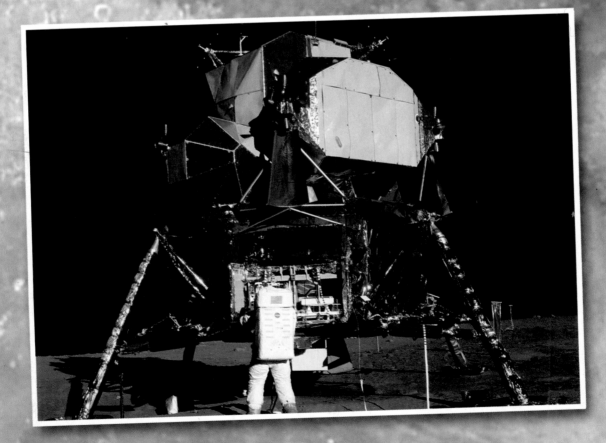

Apollo 11 was the first spacecraft to land on the Moon. This was on 20th July 1969.

The first man on the
Moon was Neil Armstrong.
He is on the left in this
photograph.

As he jumped down to the
surface, Neil Armstrong
said "It's one small step
for man, one giant leap
for mankind."

Buzz Aldrin
was the
second man
to walk on
the Moon.

Moon Landers

When the **Apollo 11** **astronauts** flew to the Moon, their spacecraft was in three parts.

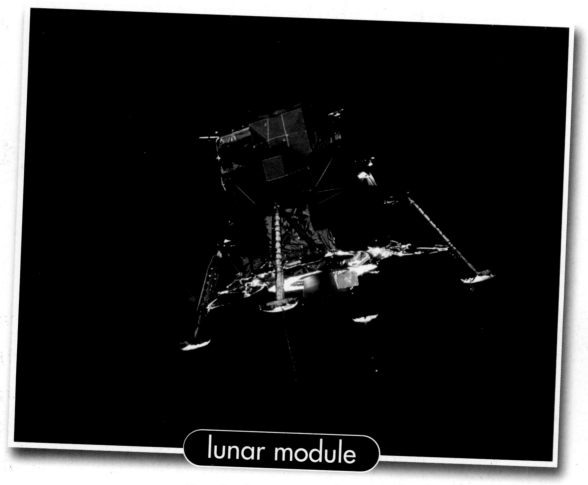

lunar module

One part travelled down to land on the Moon, carrying the astronauts Neil Armstrong and Buzz Aldrin. This was the lunar module, called Eagle.

The other two parts, the command module and the service module, stayed in **orbit** around the Moon. The command module was called Columbia.

command module

Earth

Moon

Eagle

When the mission was over, the lunar module took off using its own rockets. It joined on to the command module. Then the spacecraft carried the astronauts back to Earth.

Travel and Life on the Moon

The last mission to the Moon was **Apollo** 17 in 1972. The **astronauts** on Apollo 15, 16 and 17 travelled around the Moon using lunar rovers. A lunar rover is often called a 'Moon buggy'.

This is a photograph of the Lunar Rover on the surface of the Moon.

The top speed of the Lunar Rover was 13 km per hour.

The Moon buggy was very light. It could travel across the Moon's surface carrying the astronauts and all the rocks they collected.

Scientists would like to build a place on the Moon where people could live for many months.

Will there be a **moonbase** in your lifetime?

Glossary

Apollo A project of missions to the Moon between 1963 and 1972. Its aim was to land a human on the Moon and get them back to Earth safely. There were 17 Apollo missions, but only 6 successfully landed on the Moon.

Asteroid A rocky object that orbits the Sun. Most asteroids orbit the Sun between Mars and Jupiter.

Astronauts People trained to travel or work in space.

Astronomers People who study space, often using telescopes.

Atmosphere The gases that surround a star, planet or moon.

Craters Holes in the surface of a planet or a moon. They are made either by a volcano or when a rock from space crashes into the surface and leaves a deep dent.

Comets Objects usually made of ice and frozen gas that are in orbit around the Sun.

Earth days A day is the time it takes a planet to spin around once. A day on Earth is 24 hours long.

Moonbase A place on the Moon that scientists may build one day.

Humans would be able to live there for many months.

Orbit The path planets or other objects take around the Sun, or satellites take around planets.

Satellites Moons or man-made objects that orbit around a planet.

Solar system The Sun and everything that is in orbit around it.

Tides The change of the height of the surfaces of oceans. This change happens about every 12 hours.

Index

Apollo missions 18–23

astronauts 19-20

astronomers 10–11

atmosphere 6

craters 8–9, 11, 17

Eagle (lunar module) 20

earth 14

far side 10–11

full moon 13

landers 20–1

'Moon Buggy' 22

moonbase 17, 23

new moon 13

north pole (moon) 16

orbit 5, 14–15, 21

planets 4–5

shape changes 12–13

size 7

south pole (moon) 16

spacecraft 20, 22–3

temperature 9

tides 14–15

travel 22–3

water 16